MOWGLI'S SONS

KIPLING AND BADEN-POWELL'S SCOUTS

HUGH BROGAN

JONATHAN CAPE

THIRTY-TWO BEDFORD SQUARE LONDON

First published 1987
Copyright © 1987 by Hugh Brogan
Jonathan Cape Ltd, 32 Bedford Square, London WC1B 3EL

British Library Cataloguing in Publication Data

Brogan, Hugh
Mowgli's sons: Kipling and Baden-Powell's scouts.
1. Baden-Powell, Robert Baden-Powell, *Baron* –
Friends and associates   2. Kipling, Rudyard –
Contemporaries   3. Great Britain, *Army* –
Biography   4. Generals – Great Britain –
Biography   5. Authors, English – Biography
I. Title
369.43'092'4   DA68.32.B2

ISBN 0–224–02451–5
ISBN 0–224–02460–4 Pbk

Printed in Great Britain by
Butler & Tanner Ltd
Frome and London

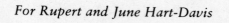

For Rupert and June Hart-Davis

CONTENTS

ILLUSTRATIONS

ACKNOWLEDGMENTS

This book is being published thanks to the loyal support of Jonathan Cape and the generosity of the University of Sussex, which presented me with the Ralph Lewis award. Books selected for that award have to have some Sussex connection, and in 1986, the fiftieth anniversary of Rudyard Kipling's death, it was thought proper to make a special Kipling presentation.

I owe thanks to many other people: to Mr John McGivering, of the Kipling Society, who asked me to read a paper to the Society, of which invitation *Mowgli's Sons* is the result; to the members of the Kipling Society, who listened to my talk with singular patience and good humour and afterwards offered many helpful comments, which have enabled me notably to improve this essay; to Mr John Burt, of the University of Sussex Library, who gave me every assistance when I needed to consult the Kipling Papers; to Miss Elizabeth Rodger, the University of Sussex Librarian, for many kindnesses; to the Royal Commonwealth Society, where the Kipling Society's library is housed; to the National Trust, for permission to quote from the Kipling Papers; to Mr G. A. Coombe, archivist of the Scout Association, for making my visits to Baden-Powell House so pleasant; to the Scout Association itself, for permission to quote copyright Baden-Powell material; to the present Lord Baden-Powell and to Mr R. C. Taylor, the curator of Kipling's house, Bateman's, for their replies to my letters; and not least to my colleague at the University of Essex, Dr G. A. Crossick, for giving me a useful list of monographs to read when I first began to take an interest in the subject of Scouting.

I would like to thank the Scout Association for permission to reproduce plates 2, 3, 4 and 6 (numbers 3 and 4 are from *Sketches*

Acknowledgments

in Mafeking, and number 6 is from *The Scouter*) and the cover of 'All Patrols Look Out' and Baden-Powell's letter to Kipling, and the Hulton Picture Library for plates 1, 5, and 7.

Wivenhoe, St Hugh's Day, 1986   HUGH BROGAN

1
MEN OF EMPIRE

Britain in the late nineteenth century was a once-rural country trying to come to terms with the fact that she had become an urban one. The process of adjustment had been going on for the greater part of the century. Some fundamental rearrangements had been made, and urban culture was evolving rapidly. But there remained much to be done if the new cities were to be truly civilised. Britain had grown too big, too complex, to be accurately summed up in one phrase, or even in two. A multiplicity of influences were at work, and a multiplicity of attitudes found vigorous expression in books, in art, in sermons, in journalism and in political speeches. Nevertheless it may safely be asserted that to intelligent young men brought up in genuinely artistic or intellectual or public-spirited homes there was nothing in Britain, whatever her strength and success, to silence criticism. Rather the reverse: the triumphant vigour of the country made the duty of trying to correct her faults all the more imperative, for it bred a sense that all things were possible. The great work of the preceding generation – of men and women such as the sanitary reformer, Edwin Chadwick, Florence Nightingale, and W. E. Forster, author of the 1870 Education Act – showed what could be done. The only question was, where to start? And the answer to that depended on where you started yourself.

If you were a child of the new city, you might turn out to be a Bernard Shaw. His first forty years were spent entirely in Dublin and London. Such being his horizons, it is scarcely surprising that he thought of the St Pancras vestry, of which he became a member, as more than sufficient training in practical politics. His teetotalism, vegetarianism, pure wool clothes, obsession with fresh air and absolute distrust of doctors were so many acts of rebellion against the life-shortening conditions of the new urbanism; they were assertions that it was possible to be healthy and humane even in a city where you were constantly threatened by alcohol, soot and adulterated food. His critique was that of an insider. So, on the whole, was that of the earnest young men and women of that era when, as H. W. Nevinson remarked, 'society was seized by one of its brief and fitful fevers for doing good'.[1] They flung themselves, if not into the Fabian

[1] Quoted by John Springhall, *Youth, Empire And Society: British youth movements, 1883–1940* (London, 1977), p. 45.

15

Society, at least into Toynbee Hall, university settlements, public school missions and, in due course, the various boys' organisations which sought through military training to rescue city urchins from the horrors of the street corner, the public house, and cigarettes.

Rudyard Kipling and Robert Baden-Powell approached the urban world as outsiders. They might well have directed at Shaw personally Kipling's famous question, 'What should they know of England who only England know?' They learned to worry about the problem of the city from having concerned themselves with the problem of the military security of the British Empire (Baden-Powell was never tired of citing the appalling numbers of volunteers in the Second Boer War and in 1914 who proved to be physically unfit for soldiering).[1] They brought to their country a vision that was less agile, less urbane, possibly less acute than Shaw's; but it was also wider and, crucially, more imaginative.

Their lives followed an oddly similar pattern. If, in Fulham, little Rudyard was told the story of Burnt Njal by William Morris, sitting on a rocking-horse, then in Kensington, not many years earlier, John Ruskin had assured little Robert's mother that her son's ambidexterity was nothing to worry about. There were important resemblances between their schools. Kipling has given various accounts of his experiences at the United Services College, most strikingly in *Stalky & Co.*; how close the U.S.C. ethos was to that of Baden-Powell's Charterhouse can be gathered from the following passage, in which B-P (as he was always known) describes his habitual truancy in a wood near the school:

As a trapper I set my snares, and when I caught a rabbit or hare (which wasn't often) I learned by painful experience to skin, clean and cook him. But knowing that Redskins were about, in the shape of masters looking for boys out of bounds, I used a very small non-smoking fire for fear of giving away my whereabouts. Incidentally, also, I gained sufficient cunning to hide up in trees when danger of this kind threatened, since

---

[1] According to various official sources, approximately 60 per cent of the male population were, in the opening years of the century, unfit for military service. This finding caused widespread alarm.

experience told me that masters hunting for boys seldom looked upward.[1]

Compare this with the opening of *Stalky & Co.*:

In summer all right-minded boys built huts in the furze-hill behind the College – little lairs whittled out of the heart of the prickly bushes, full of stumps, odd root-ends, and spikes, but, since they were strictly forbidden, palaces of delight. And for the fifth summer in succession, Stalky, M'Turk, and Beetle (this was before they reached the dignity of a study) had built like beavers a place of retreat and meditation, where they smoked ... Providence moved Mr. Prout, whose school-name, derived from the size of his feet, was Hoofer, to investigate on his own account; and it was the cautious Stalky who found the track of his pugs on the very floor of the lair one peaceful afternoon when Stalky would fain have forgotten Prout and his works in a volume of Surtees and a new briar-wood pipe.[2]

Both Kipling and Baden-Powell were pitched straight from school into work in the Indian Empire, and the early years of the twentieth century found both of them settling down in an England which neither had lived in continuously for many years. The Second Boer War was a crucial experience for each of them.

What all this proves is not that there was a mysterious destiny at work, but that each man was a child of his times.

And there was one important difference in their experience. There was nothing in B-P's life comparable to the House of Desolation at Southsea, where the child Kipling, abandoned, it seemed, by his parents, and helpless against his persecutors, learned some lessons about the grimness of life and the stoicism required to endure it that Baden-Powell never absorbed.

The two men first met in Lahore, between October 1882 (when Kipling began his work there as a journalist) and November

---

[1] William Hillcourt, *Baden-Powell: the two lives of a hero* (London, 1964), p. 29.
[2] Rudyard Kipling, *Stalky & Co.* (London, 1899), pp. 1–2.

1884 (when Baden-Powell left India). They met through their relations: 'His father and my eldest brother were colleagues in establishing the Museum in Lahore of Indian arts and crafts.'[1] Thus B-P in his memorial notice of Kipling for *The Scouter*. He says no more, and no other source known to me mentions the connection. We can only speculate as to whether B-P at the time seemed anything more than a commonplace pig-sticking, polo-playing, amateur-acting subaltern, or Kipling more than a brash if promising cub reporter, not yet out of his teens. Both young men had an enormous zest for life, which may have created a bond; but B-P cannot have been in Lahore very often (he was stationed at Muttra, south of Delhi) and it is probably best to take literally his statement that he did not get to know Kipling well until they met again in Cape Town in 1901. In the interval both men became world-famous.

Kipling, in his autobiography, stated firmly that in his 'working life' he had merely played the cards that were dealt him.[2] His modesty about his literary gifts was one of his noblest traits, and we can be sure that it was the genuine article because it spoke the truth. Kipling *was* lucky in the place and hour of his arising. The British Empire was in some ways so new. The Indian Mutiny had been a turning-point. It had given British rule in India a heroic colouring. It had led to a great strengthening of the British presence, both military and civilian. Next, the need to protect the road to India had led to imperial expansion in Africa. Then the need to escape from Britain and to people the white colonies in Canada, Australia and New Zealand had led to government-encouraged emigration. By the 1880s a transformed Empire was a matter of fresh interest to the British (we need not enter into the question of exactly how many felt this interest, for the number was surely huge); and it had never been exploited for literature. Enter a young writer of genius, and the thing was done. Yet how much that young writer owed to circumstances can perhaps be suggested by the fact that Baden-Powell, an impecunious junior officer, forced to supplement his pay as best he could, also found a ready market for the sketches, stories

---

[1] *The Scouter*, March 1936, p. 82. The brother in question was Baden Henry Powell, judge of the chief court at Lahore.
[2] Rudyard Kipling, *Something Of Myself* (London, 1937), p. 1.

and articles that he poured forth so readily with his left and right hands. He was Kipling's inferior as a writer, just as he was his superior as a draughtsman; but his writings on military and colonial life brought him in a good income, just as if he had been a literary genius too.

If the cards were good, Kipling played them superbly. He established himself as the Empire's chief, in a sense its only, writer. It is unnecessary to itemise the works which won him innumerable readers, for whom he brought all parts of the Empire to life, and which made him an incalculable cultural influence. But three of his books require mention here. In *The Jungle Books* and the figure of Mowgli he conceived a myth of abiding fascination, whose appeal far transcended the elements of superficial allegory in the stories realising it. *Stalky & Co.* was a lesser work, but in it Kipling let loose a spirit of Misrule, or perhaps rather of Unrule, that offered little support for the solemnities of imperial institutions.[1] And in *Kim*, his farewell to India, the principal theme was a question of choice: should Kim become a mere agent of Empire, a pawn in the Great Game, or should he follow the lama in the greater Way of the Buddha? To some degree this theme expressed the author's own predicament. Kipling, a hugely imaginative man, was constantly tempted to subordinate imagination to the pedestrian demands of everyday life: to send Mowgli to work as a forester for the government. But the artist in him could never finally surrender to the utilitarian. In 'The Spring Running' Mowgli may leave the jungle, but Kipling and his readers do not.

Towards the end of the 1890s Kipling invented Baden-Powell. I mean more by this than that 1899 was the year both of *Stalky* and of the siege of Mafeking. To be sure, Baden-Powell was the true Stalky (I mean no disrespect to the memory of Kipling's schoolfellow, General Dunsterville); it was his brilliantly off-beat leadership which best vindicated Kipling's belief that:

India's full of Stalkies – Cheltenham and Haileybury and Marlborough chaps – that we don't know anything about,

---

[1] I have discussed *Stalky & Co.* at greater length in 'Stalky and Kipling', *Kipling Journal*, nos. 176–7 (December 1970, March 1971).

and the surprises will begin when there is a really big row on.[1]

More important, Kipling's verse and prose had for twelve years been telling the British public what to expect of its modestly heroic regiments; at Mafeking Baden-Powell and his men vindicated a dream, the more beguilingly because of the failures of all the other imperial forces in South Africa. It is really not surprising that a wave of patriotic love washed over the brave and successful commander. This was the happy warrior that every boy in England (taught by Kipling) longed to be.

Yet if the poet of Empire had opened the way for B-P, he too, though a much simpler man, had played his cards brilliantly. Mafeking was a professional challenge that he had prepared himself deliberately to meet. He had for years held a poor opinion of the British army's training, and in a stream of pamphlets had argued for improvements. His speciality was field reconnaissance; Mafeking was his chance to vindicate his theories, which he did completely. But if the siege made him a national hero, it did nothing to endear him to orthodox military circles, where he was regarded as a dangerous eccentric who had never been to Staff College. As such he was excluded from all the really important army positions, where the planning for Armageddon was taking place, in the years following the peace in South Africa.[2]

Indeed B-P, though he does not appear yet to have suspected it, was in 1901 nearing the turning-point of his career. His sudden celebrity, which had been eagerly megaphoned by the press, had naturally drawn attention to his writings, among them his latest pamphlet, *Aids To Scouting For NCOs And Men*, the corrected proofs of which left Mafeking in the last mail before the siege began. Boys who got their hands on the book found in it the rudiments of a fascinating new game. Social workers discovered a scheme of training which might work wonders for the children of crowded, mean, urban dwellings. A desire got abroad to emulate the boys of Mafeking, whom Major

---

[1] *Stalky & Co.*, p. 271.
[2] Winston S. Churchill, *Great Contemporaries* (London: revised edition, 1938), p. 365.

Lord Edward Cecil had formed into an effective auxiliary troop. Fan mail poured over the sea to General Baden-Powell.

To Kipling he must at first have been interesting chiefly as a commander against the Boers. Kipling himself, as a journalist, as the friend of Cecil Rhodes, and as the administrator of the 'Absent-Minded Beggar' Fund, which provided tobacco, pyjamas, and other such comforts for the troops, had been in the thick of things in 1900. The military lessons of the war and its early disasters were much on his mind: after a summer and autumn in England he had returned to South Africa in the early winter, and spent the voyage out in writing 'The Army Of A Dream', the weightiest, though not, artistically, the most successful of a group of tales he wrote at about this time on the theme of military training.[1] One of the best of them was 'The Way That He Took', which was eventually collected in *Land And Sea Tales*. It seems in part to be a tribute to Mary Kingsley, the African traveller, whom Kipling called 'the bravest woman of all my knowledge'.[2] She had died while nursing Boer prisoners in a military hospital at Simons Town. But the tale also contains a vivid exposition of the value of careful scouting on the veldt, a subject much in Kipling's mind just then because of a fearfully successful Boer ambush at Sanna's Post, outside Bloemfontein.[3] It is inconceivable that when Kipling met the British Army's leading authority on scouting, as we know from Mrs Kipling's diary that he did, he did not pick his brains thoroughly on the subject.[4]

Yet there is one curious indication that perhaps Kipling also

[1] Charles Carrington, *Rudyard Kipling: his life and work* (London, 1955), p. 315.
[2] Kipling, *Something Of Myself*, p. 77. It may be pointed out in passing that Kipling has slightly falsified his anecdote of Mary Kingsley. He has her holding forth on West African cannibals four years before her first African journey.
[3] See Carrington, *op. cit.*, pp. 311–12. Mary Kingsley died on 3 June 1900; 'The Way That He Took' was published in the *Daily Express* on the 12th and 13th June.
[4] Mrs Kipling's diary recorded two visits by Baden-Powell to 'The Woolsack' (Kipling's house in Cape Town) on 19 March and 2 April 1901. See Charles Carrington, 'Extracts From The Diaries Of Mrs Rudyard Kipling' (typescript). Copies deposited with the Kipling Society and the Royal Commonwealth Society.

gathered from Baden-Powell which way the wind was blowing for him in England. He may even, at this date or a little later, have read *Aids To Scouting*. The evidence prompting this guess is the belated Just-So story, 'The Tabu Tale', which was published in the *Windsor Magazine* in September 1903. Tegumai and Taffimai appear again, but the story is unworthy of them. The baby-talk of its narrative style lacks conviction. However, its matter reads like a tract for the Boy Scouts who did not yet exist: Taffy learns the elements of woodcraft, and though Kipling may have learned about the art from the writings of Ernest Thompson Seton, which were beginning to appear in America, it is surely as likely that he did so from Baden-Powell.[1] If so, 'The Tabu Tale' is prophetic, whatever its artistic weaknesses. It may even be something more. It suggests the possibility that Kipling gave ideas to B-P as well as taking them from him. If so, he can claim to be one of the originators of the Boy Scout movement.

These matters would be clearer if we had any but the barest information about the 1901 re-encounter between the long-sundered friends. We can at least be sure that on a personal level the meeting was a success. The two men never quite lost touch again, and when B-P (who had meanwhile been appointed Inspector-General of Cavalry in England) returned to South Africa in 1906, in the train of Joseph Chamberlain, he and Kipling met on the warmest terms. B-P made a rather unsatisfactory drawing of Kipling, and showed him a sketch of the sky and the ocean which he made on his voyage. Kipling at first held it upside down, and thought he was looking at a sketch of the veldt with a storm coming up overhead. When he discovered (or was told) his mistake, he scribbled down a verse on a matchbox to commemorate the incident:

> This is the ocean bright and blue
> That the *Armadale Castle* plowtered through,
> But if you turn it the other way
> It's the lonely veldt on a cloudy day,
> That is if you hold it upside down

---

[1] Seton's *The Birchbark Roll Of The Woodcraft Indians* had a great influence on Baden-Powell, but did not appear until 1906.

It's the gathering storm on the desert brown;
And very seldom since Art begun
Could you get two pictures by drawing one.[1]

This is impressive only as an example of Kipling's facility; but it is interesting as the nearest we ever get to his informal relations with Baden-Powell. The rest of the evidence always shows them in what may be called semi-official attitudes to each other. At least this scrap of doggerel goes a little way to conveying to us the warm friendship which B-P saluted feelingly at the end of his long life. And with it we may associate Kipling's daughter Elsie's memory that on the family's annual voyage out to South Africa in the early years of the century old friends were often on board: 'Dr. Jameson, Abe Bailey, Baden-Powell, mining engineers, and many of the big men who were shaping the destiny of South Africa at that time; endless talks and deck pacing went on in their company.'[2] Perhaps it was during one of these talks that the incident of the picture and the matchbox occurred.

The South African war and its aftermath made a period of stocktaking for Kipling. His prose works on this theme were some of the dullest things he ever wrote: few will ever name 'The Army Of A Dream', or 'The Comprehensions Of Private Cooper' or 'The Captive' among their favourite Kipling short stories. But when he tackled the same themes in verse he was at his most masterly. Not only did he rub in what he took to be the lessons of the war quite unmercifully, but he achieved that rarest of all things in English poetry, really memorable and permanently valuable political verse:

Me that 'ave been what I've been –
Me that 'ave gone where I've gone –
Me that 'ave seen what I've seen –
   'Ow can I ever take on
With awful old England again,
An' 'ouses both sides of the street,

[1] Robert Baden-Powell, *Sketches In Mafeking And East Africa* (London, 1907), p. 5.
[2] Carrington, *Rudyard Kipling*, p. 384.

And 'edges two sides of the lane,
And the parson an' gentry between,
An' touchin' my 'at when we meet –
Me that 'ave been what I've been?

Or,

If England was what England seems,
An' not the England of our dreams,
But only putty, brass, an' paint,
'Ow quick we'd chuck 'er! But she ain't!

Or,

It was our fault, and our very great fault, and *not* the judgment
of Heaven.
We made an Army in our own image, on an island nine by
seven,
Which faithfully mirrored its makers' ideals, equipment, and
mental attitude –
And so we got our lesson: and we ought to accept it with
gratitute.

Or, above all, 'The Islanders':

Yet ye were saved by a remnant (and your land's long-
suffering star)
When your strong men cheered in their millions while your
striplings went to the war.
Sons of the sheltered city – unmade, unhandled, unmeet –
Ye pushed them raw to the battle as ye picked them raw from
the street.
And what did ye look they should compass? Warcraft learned
in a breath.
Knowledge unto occasion at the first far view of Death?
So? And ye train your horses and the dogs ye feed and prize?
How are the beasts more worthy than the souls, your sacrifice?

Kipling said all this in prose and in verse, over and over again;
in one form or another he issued warnings in the same strain,

as occasion required, for the rest of his life. This prophetic vein was to have a crucial bearing on his future relations with Baden-Powell.

For B-P's return to England from the war in 1903 proved to be the most momentous event of its kind since Florence Nightingale came back from the Crimea. It was already clear to all who took an interest in such things that something new was afoot. It was not just that *Aids To Scouting* had been so successful, or that Baden-Powell's immense popularity showed no signs of diminishing or quietening. A new ethos was establishing itself. In poetry, the way was opening for the Georgians: dog-roses were replacing green carnations, beer was replacing absinthe, and as Yeats was to remark, 'everybody got down off his stilts'.[1] It was not only a matter of poetry. The Boer War had vitalised the message of Empire, associating it (not least in Kipling's work) with wide skies and clean air. It was not only a matter of war. Traces of it can be found wherever we look in these years. Even Bernard Shaw went to live in the country. And this new ethos left a deep mark on children's literature. For example, in 1909 E. Nesbit was to publish *Harding's Luck*. No one who has ever read it will forget the superb opening chapters and the contrast they paint between the life of the Deptford slums and the life of a tramp on the Kentish roads, still less the wonder of going to sleep in the Bed With Green Curtains:

> And in the morning the birds wake you, and you curl down warm among the hay and look up at the sky that is growing lighter and lighter, and breathe the chill, sweet air, and go to sleep again wondering how you have ever been able to lie of nights in one of those shut-up boxes with holes in them which we call houses.[2]

We find the same feeling in the opening of *Rewards And Fairies*, which came out in the following year:

> It was their first summer in boots, and they hated them, so they took them off, and slung them round their necks, and

---

[1] W. B. Yeats, *The Oxford Book Of Modern Verse* (Oxford, 1936), p. xi.
[2] E. Nesbit, *Harding's Luck* (London, 1947 edition), pp. 35–6.

paddled joyfully over the dripping turf where the shadows lay the wrong way, like evening in the East.

And in this same period Arthur Ransome was learning all the outdoor skills, from making a cowslip ball to sailing a small boat, which he later put into his books. It was at this time that he pitched his 'King's Herdsmen's Tent' in Low Yewdale in the Lake District, one of the first to be seen 'in those valleys which are now thick with campers'.[1]

The subject is too large to be explored further here, but there can be no doubt that in the first years of the twentieth century many English people decided that the cure for urban woes was a return to the countryside, if only at weekends.

Into this moment came Robert Baden-Powell, looking for work which could usefully exploit what he called his 'damnable notoriety'.[2] He did not, in his heart of hearts, enjoy being a general half as much as he had liked being a regimental officer. And although, as a professional soldier, he had been appalled by the physical and mental unfitness of the recruits in the Boer War, as a humane and intelligent man he knew that what was in question was something larger than the mere military future of the country. Indeed, his Stalky side was instinctively averse to the mechanical discipline of the barrack square and the military life as conceived by most of his brother officers.

---

[1] Arthur Ransome, *Autobiography* (London, 1976), p. 128. It is perhaps surprising that Ransome never had any contact with the Scout movement, not even the Sea Scouts. The part Kipling's work played in inspiring the Scouts and Cubs was rather like that played by Ransome's stories in inspiring The Venturers Norfolk Broads Cruise, which every year teaches schoolboys and girls to sail in boats of their own on the Broads.

[2] Henry Collis *et al.*, *B.-P.'s Scouts* (London, 1961), p. 25.

2
HOW TO HOWL

There is no reason to think that B-P had been much interested in children in the past. His soldiers had taken up all his attention. However he could not ignore the hero-worship that now greeted him everywhere, and when in 1903 he was brought into contact with the Boys' Brigade he was much impressed by the enthusiasm of the boys and their trainers, and by the high standard of their training. He was rather repelled by the fact that all they did was march and manipulate dummy rifles. Furthermore, even the 54,000 members of the Brigade were not very many considering the enormous number of boys available. He told the commander, Sir William Smith, that a more attractive and varied programme ought to bring in half a million.

He asked me how I would add to its attraction, and I told him how Scouting had proved its popularity with young men in the Cavalry, and that something of the kind might prove equally attractive to these younger boys, while its aim might easily be diverted from war to peace, since the inculcation of character, health and manliness was its basis, and these qualities were as much needed in a citizen as in a soldier. He cordially agreed with my idea and suggested that I should write a book for boys on the lines of *Aids To Scouting*.[1]

B-P was too busy with his official duties to make much progress with this project during the next few years; but as he travelled round Britain he became more and more convinced that something needed to be done for the 'pale, narrow-chested, hunched-up, miserable specimens of boys and men'[2] whom he saw everywhere and who seemed to pass their time exclusively in smoking, betting and passively spectating at football matches. In 1907 he was placed on the Reserve at half-pay; he was entirely free for a year or two to bring his scouting ideas to fruition. He settled down to writing *Scouting For Boys*, which appeared in four weekly parts in January and February 1908. The first of these instalments contains a summary of *Kim*, and a game, called 'Kim's Game', based on the Lurgan episode in that book. Kipling allowed B-P to make use of this material *gratis*.

[1] Henry Collis *et al.*, *B.-P.'s Scouts* (London, 1961), p. 25.
[2] William Hillcourt, *Baden-Powell*, quoting B-P, (London, 1964), p. 251.

The summary of *Kim* is in its way a work of genius, for it manages to mention that all-important character, the lama, only as 'an old wandering priest who was tramping about India' and, in a different place, as if he were a different personage, as 'a holy priest who was struck by Russian spies'. Such distortions were the inevitable consequences of reducing a complex work of art to a mere treatise on scouting in India: B-P's last word on the book is that 'These and other adventures of Kim are well worth reading because they show what valuable work a boy scout could do for his country if he were sufficiently trained and intelligent.'[1] Such was B-P's charm, or the power of his ideas, that Kipling acquiesced in this treatment. He may even have been flattered by the ingenuity with which B-P turned the sinister game of the healer of sick pearls into a healthy test for English Boy Scouts. And at some stage he made his own original contribution to Scout lore by inventing a chant for the Scouts' rallying-song:

Be prepared! Zing-a-zing! Bom! Bom!

That is what I call entering into the spirit of things.[2]

But Kipling drew the line at writing an encouraging message for the first issue of *The Scout*, the weekly magazine for boys which B-P began to publish in April 1908. He seldom responded to such appeals, however good the cause: he disliked exploiting his reputation.[3] B-P had to make do with a message from Lord Roberts of Kandahar.

He scarcely needed it. The book, the magazine, an adroit publicity campaign, B-P's own heroic prestige, and the intrinsic appeal of the scouting idea both to boys and men, ensured that the new movement spread like a forest fire. B-P, whom the army soon put to the work of training a division of Territorials, found it hard to carry out his military duties, such were the demands of scouting upon him. But we can catch him in a moment of repose, at the end of August 1908, presiding over a fortnight's

---

[1] Robert Baden-Powell, *Scouting For Boys* (London, 1908), p. 19.
[2] B-P revealed Kipling's authorship of this 'anthem' in his obituary notice in *The Scouter*, March 1936. The words were printed in *Scouting For Boys*.
[3] See Charles Carrington, *Rudyard Kipling* (London, 1955), p. 304.

camp at Humshaugh on the Scottish Border, writing about his experience in *The Scout* in a manner which displays the lively and sensitive imagination that underlay his somewhat hearty exterior (his prose is normally rather blunt) and suggests that perhaps he had been reading or re-reading the Parnesius passages in *Puck Of Pook's Hill*:

> I sit writing this letter in the camp on the top of a great hillside overlooking the Northumbrian moors and dales; an ancient British fortress is in view on one side, the mighty Roman Wall on the other, a grey old castle below where the Moss Troopers used to fight, and the snaky continuous high road for moving the English troops against the Scots in the Jacobite times, all are there to suggest what a country of fighting and romance we are in. Every rock and dingle where we are Scouting to-day has had its Scouts there before – Scouting for their lives, in deadly earnest, many times in the last two thousand years.[1]

It was impossible that Kipling could for ever hold aloof from this sort of thing.

B-P approached him again in the early summer of 1909. That autumn the first of the great Scout rallies was to be held at the Crystal Palace, and B-P wanted a song.

The Castle,
Richmond, Yorks.

6 May 09

My dear Kipling
      Forgive me.
The Boy Scouts are 130,000 strong in Great Britain now – and are growing fast in Australia, N. Zealand, Canada, S. Africa, Germany, Denmark, Russia, America, Argentina, Chile and – Smyrna!
      I have had Boy Scouts Anthems etc. pressed on me –

---

[1] Collis, op. cit., pp. 47–8. In *The Scout*, 23 October 1909, B-P was to give an enthusiastic account of the Parnesius stories, likening Parnesius's experience of the siege of the Wall to his own at the siege of Mafeking, particularly its ending.

generally piffle or long rigmaroles high above their heads and memory.

If the spirit would move you to give them a sentiment in rhyme I can promise you it will be a very great thing for many thousands of good young hearts.

If it is a trouble or a bore – tear this up and think no more about it.

In any case please forgive my cheek in bothering you – and prove your forgiveness by lending me your son for a week or so in August to come to my Scouts Camp. I hope to make sailors of them this year by having them on board ship and practising cutting out expeditions, piracy, and Treasure Islands, etc.

Yours vy sincerely
Robert Baden-Powell.[1]

This appeal was answered handsomely. At the end of June Kipling wrote his splendid 'Boy Scouts' Patrol Song', and sent it to Baden-Powell on 5 July:[2]

These are *our* regulations –
    There's just one law for the Scout
And the first and the last, and the present and the past,
And the future and the perfect is 'Look out!'
    I, thou and he, look out!
    We, ye and they, look out!
    Though you didn't or you wouldn't
    Or you hadn't or you couldn't;
    You jolly well *must* look out!

Look out, when you start for the day,
    That your kit is packed to your mind;
There is no use going away
    With half of it left behind.
Look out that your laces are tight,
    And your boots are easy and stout,
Or you'll end with a blister at night.
    (*Chorus*) *All* Patrols look out!

[1] B-P to RK, 6 May 1909 (Kipling Papers, University of Sussex).
[2] Charles Carrington, 'Extracts from the Diaries of Mrs Rudyard Kipling' (typescript). (The Kipling Society and the Royal Commonwealth Society.)

Figure 1   The front cover of 'All Patrols Look Out'

Look out for the birds of the air,
    Look out for the beasts of the field –
They'll tell you how and where
    The other side's concealed.
When the blackbird bolts from the copse,
    Or the cattle are staring about,
The wise commander stops
    And (*chorus*) All Patrols look out!

Look out when your front is clear,
    And you feel you are bound to win.
Look out for your flank and your rear –
    That's where surprises begin.
For the rustle that isn't a rat,
    For the splash that isn't a trout,
For the boulder that may be a hat
    (*Chorus*) All Patrols look out!

For the innocent knee-high grass,
    For the ditch that never tells,
Look out! Look out ere you pass –
    And look out for everything else!
A sign mis-read as you run
    May turn retreat to a rout –
For all things under the sun
    (*Chorus*) All Patrols look out!

Look out when your temper goes
    At the end of a losing game;
When your boots are too tight for your toes;
    And you answer and argue and blame.
It's the hardest part of the Law,
    But it has to be learnt by the Scout –
For whining and shirking and 'jaw'
    (*Chorus*) All Patrols look out![1]

---

[1] Rudyard Kipling, *Verse: definitive edition* (London, 1940), pp. 273–4. As all too often, this baffling edition mis-dates the poem to 1913.

As so often with Kipling, the chief problem raised by these verses is, how on Earth did he know so much? We can take it for granted that he had read *Scouting For Boys*; B-P may well have explained things in conversation; a stray reference in a letter to his son John strongly suggests that by now he had read Ernest Thompson Seton; but in the 'Patrol Song' he seems to go beyond all second-hand sources; he plants himself at the very heart of the scouting game. Certainly B-P seems to have thought so. Overlooking Kipling's bland omission of all reference to the true, strongly ethical 'Law of the Scout', he vociferously commended the song to the readers of *The Scout*, where it was published on 18 September with a fine set of illustrations by T. P. Evans. A fortnight later the editor could suppose that 'By this time most of you will have learnt Rudyard Kipling's Patrol Song by heart.'[1]

All the same B-P hardly had a hit on his hands. By the time of Kipling's death the poem had been almost forgotten, and it is easy to see why. For all its lilt and insight the song (which is about 'you', not 'us') is not much more than the versified advice of a scoutmaster and as such is not the sort of thing that anyone would particularly enjoy singing round the camp-fire. It is curious that this point did not occur to Kipling: perhaps he was in a schoolmasterly mood that summer. He could so easily have adjusted the verses to suit the boys rather than the men who looked after them. And then there was the matter of a tune. According to Charles Carrington, Kipling had composed the song with 'A Life On The Ocean Wave' in mind, but apparently he did not pass on this important piece of information. As a result Scout headquarters was defeated by the problem of finding a tune to fit the words, which no doubt explains why the song did not appear at the Crystal Palace rally. The editor of *The Scout* appealed to his readers: could any of them think of a tune that would fit? ('If so, then write down the name of the song on a postcard and send it to me at once.') Failing that, could they contrive an original tune for it, for a prize of TWO GUINEAS? No

---

[1] *The Scout*, 2 October 1909. The editor was Henry Shaw. Kipling refers to 'B-P's Scouts' in a letter to John Kipling dated 20 January 1909: see Elliot L. Gilbert (ed.) *O Beloved Kids: Rudyard Kipling's letters to his children* (London, 1983), p. 79.

more is heard of this notion, so presumably it was unsuccessful. Eventually the 'Patrol Song' was set by E. Harcourt, and published as sheet music.[1]

In the end the Scouts made their own choice of Kipling's verse, and at the formal opening of camp-fire sing-songs and such functions recited four lines from 'The Feet Of The Young Men':

> Who hath smelt wood-smoke at twilight? Who hath heard the birch-log burning?
> Who is quick to read the noises of the night?
> Let him follow with the others, for the Young Men's feet are turning
> To the camps of proved desire and known delight!

But over time the origin of these lines was forgotten, except as a rumour, and in 1978 the Scout Association archivist had to write to the Kipling Society to enquire if they were really by Kipling.[2]

He had his first direct contact with the Scouts, as distinct from their Chief, in that same summer of 1909. At this stage B-P was still conducting large camps, they being the quickest way of spreading expert knowledge of scout skills and procedures. The 1909 camp took place in Hampshire in August. In all a hundred Scouts assembled for a fortnight, fifty of whom spent the first week at Bucklers Hard, on Lord Montague of Beaulieu's New Forest estate before changing places with the others, who had spent it on board C. B. Fry's training ship, the *Mercury*, moored near at hand. The hundred selected were those who had secured most new subscriptions to *The Scout*, but for some reason B-P chose to leaven the lump with a few boys personally invited. Among them, as we have seen, was John Kipling, just old enough for scouting, being eleven. It was a suitable holiday for him, for it was during this camp that the Sea Scouts began to emerge, as a product of B-P's project to make sailors of the boys, and John was destined for the Navy by his father. The weather was fine for most of the time, and everyone seems to

[1] Carrington, *Rudyard Kipling*, p. 416; *The Scout*, 2 October 1909.
[2] Scout Archives.

have enjoyed himself, but on the last day, when Kipling came over to collect his son and watch the concluding exercises and entertainments, it poured with rain and the outdoor show had to be cancelled. An indoor performance was hastily contrived. Many of the boys enjoyed capering round in Red Indian war-bonnets, much red paint and little else; but as a finale it was slightly disappointing. John Kipling does not appear to have gone scouting again.[1]

We hear no more of any direct contact with the movement for some years, but Kipling was never a writer to waste material that had come his way. In his Pyecroft story, 'The Horse Marines', published in 1911, he introduced a troop of Scouts (libellously dubbed the Pink Eye Patrol by Pyecroft) holding up all travellers into Portsmouth on the grounds that they might be enemy invaders. 'I had read of wild doings occasionally among the Boy Scouts on the Portsmouth Road, in which Navy, Army, and the world at large seemed to have taken part,' says Kipling; on this occasion the wild doings include a mobbing of Pyecroft and his friends in revenge for a walloping administered to a Scout called Eddy. Pyecroft's view of the Scouts and their scoutmasters is decidedly hostile ('they'd have scalped us, but for the intervention of an umpire – also in short under-drawers. A fleshy sight!') but a careful reading of the episode shows that Kipling himself approves of them. He likes their zeal, and their skill at the Morse code, and the general chaos they create. As Pyecroft says, 'few equatorial calms are to be apprehended when B.P.'s little pets take to signallin' ', and no one likes an equatorial calm.[2]

The year after 'The Horse Marines' Kipling, explaining Christmas holiday arrangements to his son, writes that 'on Monday night' (which must be 16 December) he will be dining in the House of Commons with Stanley Baldwin, and the next afternoon 'Mother and I may go to see General Baden-Powell.'[3] In other words, they had been invited to B-P's wedding reception

---

[1] The Bucklers Hard Camp is described by H. Geoffrey Elwes in the *Essex County Standard* of 28 August and 4 September 1909.
[2] Rudyard Kipling, *A Diversity Of Creatures* (London, 1952 edition), pp. 307–10.
[3] Gilbert, (ed.) *op. cit.,* p. 144. RK to John Kipling, 12 December 1912.

at Mercers Hall. It is to be hoped that they went. There was a guard of honour of West London Scouts, and a Scout choir entertained the guests with songs.[1] Next year, after a honeymoon in Algeria (during which B-P discovered with joy that his darling Olave was a born camper), the Baden-Powells settled at Ewhurst Place, in Robertsbridge, only ten miles or so from Kipling's home in Burwash. As they were such near neighbours it was natural that the friendship of the two men now reached its height.

Yet their lives were moving in different trajectories. B-P, a young married man of fifty-six, soon found himself also a father: his son Peter was born a year to the day after his parents' wedding and was followed in the next few years by two daughters. The Scout movement swept onwards, fanning the Chief's highest hopes for it:

> It needs no great strength of the imagination to see in this the promise of a closer bond between ourselves and our Empire across the Seas, and a stronger guarantee of future peace between nations when their men begin to look upon each other as members of one brotherhood instead of as hereditary enemies.[2]

The outbreak of war in 1914 was not an unmitigated disaster for him even though it checked the dream of international brotherhood. B-P had resigned from the army some years earlier, largely because scouting was more fun than soldiering, so he was free to throw all his energies into making his boys useful to their country. They did gratifyingly well, the Sea Scouts especially; and it was sadly splendid that among the dead in battle were no fewer than 10,000 former Scouts. Eleven were awarded the Victoria Cross. In spite of the disappearance of most of the scoutmasters into the services the organisation emerged from its ordeal stronger than before. Decidedly B-P had a good war. But these were the darkest years of Kipling's life.

---

[1] Hillcourt, *op. cit.,* p. 338.
[2] B-P's introduction to the souvenir book of the 1913 Birmingham Scout Exhibition; quoted by Hillcourt, *op. cit.,* p. 343.

Before the war he had been working himself into a dead-end with his sterile, bitter, partisan polemics over the Irish question, in a vein more common among French than English writers. Then came the threat to 'all we have and are', and John Kipling's death in battle on 27 September 1915. Kipling was only forty-nine, but from that dreadful day he began to be an old man.

B-P did not forget him that Christmas. On 23 December Kipling wrote to him:

> Many thanks for your letter and for the Christmas card from the children. I entirely agree with what you say about Education *except* that there exists a residue of Ultimate Dirt – say 5% – which *must* be coerced by fear at the beginning. Later it learns honour and responsibility.
>
> But you see we haven't had any education up to date – only a little state instruction given on rotten political lines. But I mustn't let my indignation bore you. With every good wish for your good work.[1]

It is tantalising to know so little about the context of this letter. The one from B-P to which it replies has disappeared. As all too often I must resort to conjecture. Fortunately the broad lines of the issues are impossible to mistake, even if the details are lost.

B-P presumably knew of John Kipling's death. If so it was a nice touch to attribute the Christmas card to Peter (aged two) and Heather (six months): for a moment Kipling could look away from the desolation of his own world to one which still knew happiness. But B-P was the Chief Scout as well as Kipling's friend, and he had much on his mind. Proposals were afoot to train all the boys of Britain for war by making cadets of them, which B-P felt bound to resist, partly because his Scouts were already showing themselves more than sufficiently adaptable, steady, efficient and devoted; partly because he fundamentally objected to the principles of cadet training. He wrote a pamphlet, *Cadet Training And Education*, 'for private circulation only',

---

[1] RK to B-P, 23 December 1915 (Kipling Papers, University of Sussex).

in which he set out his views. It was a credo for his scoutmasters, but he may very well have sent a copy, or a summary of his views, to Kipling. The latter's letter looks like a comment on such passages as the following:

> The accepted military discipline of obedience from fear of punishment is not the true discipline that stands the test of service, namely the subordination of self to the higher sense of duty and 'playing the game'; drill that destroys initiative and makes a man a machine is out of date in these days where intelligent co-operative action is so essential. Physical development is not attained in a few minutes of occasional 'setting up' drill, but by consistent intelligent self-development: endurance is not obtained by test marches, but by a foundation of good physical soundness. Where our men have shown up well in this crisis, has been in the splendid spirit and courage of those who have enlisted and gone to the front ... proving that our material is excellent and only needs bringing out.[1]

Kipling and Baden-Powell had much in common, but you do not have to spend long with either to discover that it was the general who was the man of peace, concerned to train boys for civilian life, believing in human goodness and the power of loving leadership to bring it out; the writer who took a dark view of humanity ('the Ultimate Dirt') and its prospects, and who valued the Scout movement largely because it prepared boys for war. This last heresy was one that gave B-P a great deal of trouble, particularly with the Labour Party (then, as now, deeply suspicious of anything new); he was constantly being accused of militarism. Friends like Kipling, or the General who said that his only purpose in becoming a Scout Commissioner was to get recruits for the Territorial Army[2] sometimes threatened to be more damaging than any enemies. Lesser differences were that Kipling always regarded the Territorial Army with disdain, and strongly, almost obsessively, believed

---

[1] This pamphlet was dated 8 July 1915 (Scout Archives).
[2] John Springhall, *Youth, Empire And Society: British youth movements, 1883–1940* (London, 1977), p. 8.

1   British Commanders in the Boer War
(Robert Baden-Powell is at the top)

2 *Above:* Howling Cubs: 16th N. Poplar (Bow Church) Wolf Cub pack, 1916

3 *Right:* A drawing of Rudyard Kipling by Baden-Powell

4 *Right:* Baden-Powell's sketch of sea and sky which Kipling mistook for a picture of the South African veldt (*above*, the right way up; *below*, upside down)

Below: Baden-Powell inspecting Wolf Cubs during the First World War

6 *Left:* Kipling with Percy Everett, Chief Scout's Commissioner, at the Jamboree held at Wembley Stadium in 1924

7 *Below:* A church service at the Scout Jamboree at Wembley, 1924, attended by The Prince of Wales

in corporal punishment in education, while B-P regarded it as 'ruinous ... since it is apt to breed braggarts, cowards, or liars amongst the youngsters'.[1]

Yet after all what united them was more important than what partially divided them; above all the child in the heart that both carried to their graves. Even here there was a contrast, between a man of action and an artist, but this doubleness was the root of their greatest joint achievement.

By 1915 the Scout movement could no longer put off the problem of what to do with all the boys under eleven years old who wanted some part in scouting. B-P was the first to acknowledge that their desire was legitimate (he remembered what he had been like himself at that age); but they could not be admitted to the patrols, partly because they were not strong enough for the full range of activities, partly because the Scouts proper did not want to associate with younger boys. B-P always stuck to this point, but the demand for some sort of junior scout system was rising to a clamour. With fathers at war and elder brothers in the Scouts winning acclaim for their part in the national struggle it was natural for the babes to dream of glory for themselves. Junior scout groups began to spring up spontaneously, just as Boy Scout groups had done ten years previously. B-P had to give close attention to their needs. The right sort of movement, he saw, could be a welcome reinforcement to the Scouts, as well as a good thing in itself; a bad plan, equally, would cost Scouting dear. And perhaps a junior movement could do something to check the upsurge of juvenile delinquency that the war occasioned.

The Chief and his closest associates had already been turning over ideas for a year or so before the war broke out. B-P had rejected the title 'Junior Scouts'. 'We must invent a name that will appeal to the small boys ... I had originally in my mind "Wolf Cubs", or "Cubs", or "Colts", or "Young Scouts".'[2] In January 1914, a set of rules for 'Wolf Cubs or Young Scouts'

---

[1] *The Scouter*, January 1923, p. 2. B-P had no objection to corporal punishment for 'hardened criminals' who committed violence or bestiality against children. He thought the possibility of a legal flogging might act as an effective deterrent to delinquent scoutmasters.

[2] B-P to Percy Everett, 19 November 1913. Quoted in Hillcourt, *op. cit.*, p. 351.

was promulgated, with the promise that a book by the Chief would shortly follow. This book would serve the needs of the Wolf Cubs as precisely as *Scouting For Boys* had served their elders, and yet be completely distinct. The idiot-genius side of Baden-Powell soon hit on a distinctive theme. Perhaps he had begun to look forward to reading the Mowgli stories to his son Peter. More probably the phrase 'Wolf Cub' itself suggested the great idea. At any rate B-P decided to work out a programme of training and pastime for the Cubs, based on the *Jungle Books*, and by the summer of 1916 *The Wolf Cub's Handbook* was in proof. Only at this late stage did B-P approach Kipling.

28 July 1916.

Dear Kipling,

You were kind enough to give me leave (some eight years ago already) to quote your story of Kim in giving the boys a lead in becoming Boy Scouts.

We are now encouraging a junior branch of the movement under the name of Wolf Cubs for youngsters between 8 and 11, and I want to enthuse them through your Mowgli and his animal friends of the Jungle Book. Would you have any objection to my introducing it to them on the lines of the enclosed proof?

It would be a very great help to me if I may and I hope that it might also help in a small way to add to the demand for your book.

Believe me,

Yours truly,

RBP.[1]

The fact that the text had got as far as proof suggests strongly that B-P knew his man; all the same, I doubt if Kipling ever did a more generous thing than in giving permission for his work to be used in this way. He was notoriously sensitive about being quoted or exploited; and B-P actually rewrote the Mowgli tales for his own purpose and in his own wooden prose. In using

---

[1] Carbon copy (Scout Archives). The original, like almost all incoming mail, was no doubt destroyed at Bateman's after being dealt with.

the *Jungle Books* as texts for moral commentary he brutally
flattened their subtlety, eliminated all effects of light and
shade, and coarsely exposed their most delicate implications.
For example:

> *Tabaqui* was the mean sneaking jackal who tried to make
> friends with everybody by flattering them: but he only wanted
> to get scraps from them. There are lots of boys like Tabaqui
> who will sneak or suck up to others hoping to get things
> given to them instead of working for them themselves.

And

> I think that we can sometimes find boys who ought to be
> among the Bandarlog – who chatter and talk a lot and do
> very little; who are dirty and untidy; who are cowardly and
> spiteful, and who obey no laws and have no discipline such
> as the Wolf Cubs have.[1]

If this sort of thing is painful to lovers of Kipling it must have
made the author wince; but he seems not to have hesitated.
Perhaps he was entranced by the games which B-P had invented
on the basis of the *Jungle Books*, or the absurd ritual:

> The call of the pack all over the world is 'We'll do our best';
> so when your Cubmaster comes into the circle you chuck up
> your chin and, all together, you howl out – making each word
> a long yowl: 'A-Kā-lă! – We-e-e-e-ll do-o-o-o ou-u-u-r BEST.'
> Yell the word 'best' sharp and loud and short and all together.

Perhaps he responded to the wonderfully childish character
which could dream all this up on the basis of his mythology;
most certainly he understood that B-P was doing good work.
At any rate, the *Handbook* was published in December 1916,
with a handsome acknowledgment to Rudyard Kipling, 'who
has done so much to put the right spirit into our rising manhood'.
The *Handbook* had all the eccentric charm and all the success

[1] Robert Baden-Powell, *The Wolf Cub's Handbook* (London, sixth
edition, 1925), pp. 25, 30.

43

of *Scouting For Boys*, and if possible reflected B-P's own character even more faithfully; thus the emphasis on the joys of acting, of drawing and of modelling ('Model the head of a monkey, only take care you don't make it too like yourself!') are entirely characteristic and, in a book of this kind, unexpected. One of the great things about Baden-Powell was that he always thought it necessary to encourage the artist as well as the adventurer in a boy. He was also a superb organiser, and the Wolf Cub movement went ahead rapidly. By the end of 1917 there were more than 28,000 Cubs in the British Isles.

At the war's end the Baden-Powells left Robertsbridge, but B-P did not lose touch with Kipling. For one thing he occasionally had to ask permission to quote something in *The Scout*. In 1919 it was 'Big Steamers', in 1922 'The Glory Of The Garden'. Kipling always agreed readily,[1] and as readily gave his help when it was sought by N. D. Power, the Chief Wolf Cub Commissioner:

2 January 1920. Bateman's, Burwash, Sussex.
Private.
Dear Sir,
In reply to your letter of the 2nd. January, you must remember that among wolves, the Head-wolf's name is always one that can be howled easily, so as to be heard at a long distance – 'Akela', therefore, is A – *KAY* – LAR, with the accent on the second syllable which can be prolonged indefinitely. The initial A, on the other hand, is almost a grunt – 'Er'. Try this as a howl and you will see the beauty of it.

Faithfully yours,
Rudyard Kipling.[2]

Thus instructed, the Wolf Cubs next year held a rally in Hyde Park at which they gave 'the Grand Howl' to the Duke of York

---

[1] RK to B-P, 7 April 1919 an1d 29 January 1922 (Scout Archives).
[2] Scout Archives. The technique of the Howl soon gave trouble again. A few years later the *Scouter* (the monthly house-magazine for scoutmasters) was advising 'a trifle of Cockney, and howl "Haow-oo-oo!"' (*Scouter*, February 1923).

(the future King George VI) who, according to the official history of the Boy Scouts, got 'the surprise of his life'.[1] A rumour had got about among the Cubs that Mr Kipling would be present.[2] To their disappointment, he was not; but B-P, delighted with the display, wrote to him immediately afterwards:

> My dear Kipling,
>
> I attended a Rally of Wolf Cubs in Hyde Park on Saturday which proved to be an eyeopener to me as it was to the very large crowd of spectators who saw it. Had I known what it was going to be like I should certainly have ventured to send you an invitation to be present. The whole spirit and action of it was based on your Jungle Book stories and I think it would have amused you, I am sure it would have interested you, to see how these were made into a method of education for the small boys of the slums as well as the suburbs.
>
> Only the 'sixers', i.e. patrol leaders, of the Cubs were present, and these numbered some 4,000. They gave a really good display of scenes from the story of Mowgli of which I enclose a programme for your information.
>
> I should like you to have been there not only to see the show but to feel the gratification you would have done at having brought so much romance and sunshine into the lives of these boys.[3]

It may well be supposed that this letter stirred up Kipling's interest. In the autumn of the following year, 1922, he showed himself very willing to see the beauty of a Howl for himself.

The occasion was the 'Posse of Welcome' staged in the grounds of the Alexandra Palace to greet the Prince of Wales on his return from a world tour (it was just like B-P to exploit the fact that Edward was the Chief Scout of Wales to make a newsworthy event that would simultaneously please the boys and give the movement valuable publicity). Urgent invitations

---

[1] Collis, *op. cit.*, p. 83.
[2] Told me by a member of the Kipling Society who was there.
[3] Kipling Papers, Sussex. The letter is undated, but the reference to 'Saturday' makes it fairly certain that it was written on 20 or 21 June, 1921. The Hyde Park rally was held on 18 June.

THE BOY SCOUTS ASSOCIATION,

25, BUCKINGHAM PALACE ROAD,

LONDON, S. W. 1.

My dear Kipling,

I attended a Rally of Wolf Cubs in Hyde Park on
Saturday which proved to be an eyeopener to me as it was to the
very large crowd of spectators who saw it.   Had I known what it
was going to be like I should certainly have ventured to send you an
invitation to be present.   The whole spirit and action of it
was based on your Jungle Book stories and I think it would have
amused you, I am sure it would have interested you, to see how
these were made into a method of education for the small boys
of the slums as well as the suburbs.

Only the "sixers", i.e. patrol leaders, of the Cubs
were present, and these numbered some 4,000.   They gave a really
good display of scenes from the story of Mowgli of which I enclose a
programme for your information.

I should like you to have been there not only to see
the show but to feel the gratification you would have done at having
brought so much romance and sunshine into the lives of these boys.

With all good wishes,   Yours sincerely,

Robert Baden-Powell

Figure 2   A letter from Baden-Powell to Kipling, June 1921

went out from Scout headquarters to Bateman's. B-P said the
Prince wanted to meet Kipling. N. D. Power wanted to show
his gratitude for the advice about the Howl, and also for the
fact that Cub training was based on the *Jungle Books*. 'If,
therefore, you could come and hear fifteen thousand or so
grateful Cubs yelling their War cry that they will do their best,
I think you will probably enjoy it.' In face of all this kind
pressure Kipling could not refuse. On 7 October, the day of the
Posse, he was in his place.

Unfortunately it was not the place that might have been
expected, and was originally offered. The Cubs did their bit:
according to the *Manchester Guardian* twenty thousand of them
gathered round the Council Rock where the Chief Scout for
Wales stood as the Big Wolf, and gave him 'probably the biggest
howl in history'. Then they demonstrated their jungle dances,
'which highly amused the Big Wolf', and formed in lines for his
inspection.[2] But Rudyard Kipling, who would surely have been
as much amused as the Prince, was stuck away in a marquee
beside the lake in the Alexandra Park, waiting with other bigwigs
(Lady Baden-Powell in Girl Guide uniform among them) for
Edward's arrival. Kipling stood out incongruously among all
the Scout hats and bare knees, for he was wearing formal dress
and a top hat. Perhaps he had not quite grasped the precise
nature of the occasion. He certainly affected to be bewildered
by it. He was given a Scout for an escort, 'whom he declared he
would not allow out of his sight until he was safely piloted out
of the Palace grounds.'[3]

He enjoyed himself, even if he missed the Cubs. The Sea
Scouts exploited the lake to demonstrate boat-building and life-
saving skills and a rescue from a shipwreck and hauling each
other across the water on ropes. A Scout fire brigade put out a
fire. The Prince was given a ceremonial row of at least thirty
yards. He inspected an élite of King's Scouts and foreign visitors
and after mounting the saluting base witnessed one of the Scouts'
most famous effects: the whole assembly (more than sixty thou-

---

[1] N. D. Power to RK, 21 September 1922 (Scout Archives).
[2] *Manchester Guardian*, 20 October 1922.
[3] Sidney Dark, in E. K. Wade, *Twenty-One Years Of Scouting* (London,
1929), pp. 255–6.

sand boys) rushed towards him, waving flags, yelling patrol cries, and brandishing their hats on the end of their scout staves. Then, just as they looked certain to overrun the base, they suddenly stopped, and listened in respectful silence to the Prince's speech. The day ended with cheers for the Prince and the King, 'Land Of Our Fathers', and the National Anthem. Kipling told Lady Baden-Powell that he had been deeply impressed by it all. She informed her husband, who wrote to Kipling in what was becoming a familiar vein:

> I cannot tell you how glad I was that you were able to be present at the 'Posse of Welcome' to the Prince of Wales on Saturday last. I look upon you as the inspirer of a lot of the spirit that exists in Scouting to-day and therefore I was glad that you should see it in practice.
>
> My wife has told me how interested you were in what you saw of it. But this was, of course, only a Posse or representative group of the whole and gave only a partial impression of its possibilities. I want to get you some day to come and see the mainspring – our School of training for Scoutmasters in Epping Forest. This would I think interest you still further and give you a new vision of our possibilities. I should like very much to tell you results that have already come and which lie deeper than those that you saw on the surface, but I cannot bore you with all this in a letter. They speak to me of greater possibilities which lie before the movement yet if only we could get on a footing for developing them.
>
> This as usual means money. Now here you could – if you *would* – give us material help, only I dare not ask you.
>
> What I want is a letter from you to the 'Times' to the people of Britain to ask their big-fisted help for this once, and we can then go ahead on our own and do a great work towards the *prevention* of misery and crime and the promotion of sane, happy citizenhood...[1]

Kipling, as we have seen, was resistant to this sort of appeal, and the present specimen (of which I have only quoted half)

---

[1] B-P to RK, 14 October 1922 (Kipling Papers, Sussex).

does not seem to have made him break his rule. But his good will towards the movement and its Chief was strong and genuine. He did not destroy B-P's letter: after all, it was something to be told you were the inspirer of the Boy Scout spirit. Something – perhaps the letter – set him to pondering what more he might do for Scouting. In June 1923 he began to look over his scrap-book for material that might suit the book of stories for Scouts which he had decided to compile.[1]

---

[1] Carrington, 'Extracts From The Diaries Of Mrs Rudyard Kipling', entry for 18 June 1923.

3
LAND AND SEA

We have no other information about the genesis of *Land And Sea Tales*, though we might have some if Kipling's warrant as Scout Commissioner were to turn up. His appointment was promulgated in 1923, but whether it was this compliment which decided him to write the book, or advance news of the book which induced B-P to make the appointment, cannot at present be guessed. All we know is that the *Tales* appeared in November, in good time for the Christmas trade, at the knock-down price of 4/-, about half what such a book would normally have cost. Kipling wanted as many Scouts and Guides as possible to have a chance of owning a copy of this, their very own book, which proclaimed on its title-page that it was *Land And Sea Tales For Scouts And Guides, by Rudyard Kipling, Commissioner, Boy Scouts.*[1]

To judge by the number of copies that turn up in second-hand bookshops, *Land And Sea Tales* sold well. It was re-published in the pocket edition almost at once (1925) with a set of disappointing illustrations by H. R. Millar – they are not a patch on his drawings for *Puck Of Pook's Hill*, and are not to be mentioned in the same breath as his work for E. Nesbit. Perhaps Millar found the text as uninteresting as have most of Kipling's critics. On its appearance *The Scouter* welcomed it enthusiastically and gratefully: 'just the sort of yarn we want for the camp-fire or the powwow at Troop headquarters'. The *Times Literary Supplement* greeted it rather more perceptively: 'A moral runs through all these stories; but Mr. Kipling, as we know, prides himself on possessing two separate sides to his head, and we are not always clear whether it is obedience or disobedience that is inculcated; perhaps the two are identical.'[2] Since then, those who have had anything to say about the book

---

[1] This title caused some embarrassment to Kipling's American publishers, in part, presumably, because in the United States the distaff wing of the movement is known as the Girl Scouts, not the Girl Guides. So the first edition was entitled *Land And Sea Tales For Boys And Girls*, the second, *For Scouts And Scoutmasters*. There is also a small mystery about RK's Scout office. According to himself he was a Boy Scout Commissioner; according to the Archivist of the Scouting Association he was a Commissioner of Cubs.

[2] *The Scouter*, December 1923; *The Times Literary Supplement*, 29 November 1923.

at all (it is not even mentioned in the *Critical Heritage* volume)[1] have always been brief and sometimes dismissive.[2] I do not think that it has had its due.

Kipling worked hard at it. He took care to select tales which had clear relevance to scouting and its principles, and he provided a linking commentary to bring out their significance. He revised his piece on the Victoria Cross, originally written in 1897, to bring it up to date, and wrote one story and eight sets of verses expressly for the book. The result is a volume with a flavour all its own, instantly distinguishable from such a hotch-potch as, say, *Abaft The Funnel*, although that too was composed – entirely composed – of material that Kipling had not previously collected.

To be sure, *Land And Sea Tales* is an uneven collection (so are several other volumes by Kipling). The material in it, in spite of the author's care, is perhaps rather too heterogeneous. But this is a small complaint, and one which comes up against the fact that tastes differ. It would probably be impossible to get general agreement as to which are the stories that weaken the collection, which those that strengthen it. They all represent the diverse aspects of Kipling's talent and achievement, about which, notoriously, opinions have always clashed. Rather than discussing the book, then, from the shaky standpoint of general literary values, I shall examine it from the Scouting point of view. How does the book appear as a contribution to Baden-Powell's beloved movement?

One point becomes instantly apparent. Kipling still had his own view of what the Boy Scouts were for, and it was not that of B-P, especially not in the 1920s. Four of the stories inculcate the virtues of good soldiering ('Winning The Victoria Cross', 'The Way That He Took', 'The Burning Of The *Sarah Sands*' and 'The Parable Of The Boy Jones'); and six of the poems embody the bleak, courageous view of life and the world which lay behind Kipling's conviction that England could not afford to neglect her defences and, especially, the training of her defenders. It was a note that he had sounded often in the pre-

[1] *Kipling: the Critical Heritage*, ed. Roger Lancelyn Green (London, 1971).
[2] See, for example, J. M. S. Tompkins, *The Art Of Rudyard Kipling* (London, 1959), p. 129.

1914 years, most notably, perhaps, in 'The Islanders'. 'The Parable Of The Boy Jones' is a work (slight enough) of that period; but it is important to note that the experience of the war has deepened and strengthened Kipling's sense of urgency. In 'The Parable' Boy Jones is persuaded that his country will need men who can handle a rifle rather than a golf-club, and sets to work on a rifle-range to learn the art. The tale is rather trite. But the poem newly attached to it is anything but trite. It is one of Kipling's prophecies. The refrain is insistent: *Vae Victis* or, as Kipling puts it, 'Woe to the weaker – woe!' 'A Departure' has to be read carefully before its full dreadful meaning comes across. It begins by evoking Hengist and his 'White Horse Banner' (where did Kipling get that detail, I wonder?) The assurance that nothing has changed on land or sea since Hengist's time does not at first seem much more than a banality, even though it is coupled with the remark that:

> Time and Tide, they are both in a tale
>   'Woe to the weaker – woe!'

The next verse too is at first sight quite comfortable, for:

> No gift can alter the grey Sea's mind,
>   But she serves the strong man well.

Are not we English strong at sea, and descendants of that strong man, Hengist? But in the next two verses our world crumbles. The pirates are shouting as they set out on their voyage, and like Hengist before them (Kipling tells us) they are coming this way:

> Hail to the first wave over the bow –
>   Slow for the sea-stroke! Slow! –
> All the benches are grunting now: –
>   'Woe to the weaker – woe!'

There must have been many scoutmasters and commissioners in the 1920s to welcome this message; but it was totally out of tune with B-P's growing internationalism. And here lies one of the saddest ironies of Scout history. Before 1914 the movement was much more nationalist than it afterwards became; it might have slowed the slither into war if it had discovered its mission of fostering international friendship a few years sooner. But in the 1920s the forces at work making for war, tyranny and revolution were far too strong for men and boys of good will. In those years Kipling's grimmer doctrines were much more apposite, and had they been heeded might have done some good. As we know, they were ignored or derided. We can only hope that some boys, reading of the heroism which won Victoria Crosses or saved the men aboard *Sarah Sands*, or learning the dedicatory verses 'Be fit! Be fit!' (I remember that in the 1950s they hung in the gymnasium at my school),[1] got something out of them of what their author intended. I would like to think that Kipling had stiffened a few of the souls who fought at Dunkirk, or El Alamein, or in Burma.

Two of the tales seem to me to have only the most tenuous connection with Scouting and the purposes of the collection as a whole. Kipling seems to have known that 'A Flight Of Fact' was a failure, to judge by the slightly apologetic note he attached to it ('it was much funnier as I heard it told by a Naval officer than it stands as I have written it from memory'). It is written and constructed on his usual lines – a tale within a tale – and his usual skill; but it does not take off, largely, I think, because a story of happy British sailors loose on a South Sea island can hardly leave out sex and retain any claim on our credulity; but Kipling was too prudish a writer, at any rate in middle age, to make more than the slightest possible passing reference to the subject. Besides, the Scout movement was notoriously obsessed with sexual purity and would not have welcomed anything which could be construed as propaganda for a different view.

The other story which does not seem to belong is 'The Son Of His Father'. It does not carry either an editorial note or a

---

[1] RK may have used B-P's remarks about 'National deterioration' (*Scouting For Boys*, 1909 edition, p. 288) as his springboard: 'History shows us, that with scarcely an exception, every great nation, after climbing laboriously to the zenith of its power, has then apparently become exhausted by the effort, and has settled down in a state of repose, relapsing into idleness and into indifference to the fact that other nations were pushing up to destroy it ... In every case the want of some of that energetic patriotism which made the country has caused its ruin.'

poem. It contains a little amateur detection by a tot of genius –
Adam, the son of Strickland the policeman – but it is unlikely
that this fact would compensate, to a Scout readership, for
the overall drift and tone of the story, which is a sentimental
celebration of childish wisdom, like 'His Majesty The King' and
'Wee Willie Winkie'. Perhaps Kipling persuaded himself that
Girl Guides would like the tale. If so I think he was wrong.

His didactic purpose in shaping the collection was strong,
and no doubt welcome to the movement. Scouting was all about
training, was avowedly supposed to be educational. But this
was hardly its essence. Winston Churchill went to the heart of
the matter when he described scouting as a means of enabling
small boys to let off steam.[1] Kipling, in his heart of hearts –
where his genius lay – knew this perfectly well, and in the other
parts of the book we see didacticism struggling with enjoyment
and usually, thank Heaven, losing.

'An Unqualified Pilot' and 'The Bold 'Prentice' are admirable
little tales, which go together, as Kipling himself pointed out.[2]
They were both published in 1895 and as to theme might well
have appeared in *The Day's Work*: but Kipling may have
thought them too slight, or too palpably written for children
('The Bold 'Prentice' first appeared in a magazine called *Youth's
Companion*). They must have been written while he was
working on the *Jungle Books* but they did not belong to
Mowgli's world, even remotely. Yet they well deserved rescuing
for book form. Their sketches of the Hugli, and of Bengal in
the monsoon, of the shipping on the river and the Indian
railways, are welcome additions to the great canvas of Kipling's
India, while the anecdotes of boyish resourcefulness are
pleasantly exciting and just within the bounds of credibility.
The verses which Kipling attached to them, 'The Junk and
the Dhow' and 'The Nurses' are splendidly vigorous and amus-
ing in themselves, and by exploring the themes of the stories
through different material give them a necessary extra weight
and authority.

Yet, if 'The Bold 'Prentice' displays a boy showing admirable
resourcefulness and disregard of self under trying conditions,

[1] Winston S. Churchill, *Great Contemporaries*, p. 367.
[2] Kipling, *Land And Sea Tales*, p. 195.

'An Unqualified Pilot', which tells how young Jim Trevor piloted a junk down the Hugli in defiance of its dangers, his father, and all regulations, scarcely sits well with the Wolf Cub insistence that 'the Cub gives in to the Old Wolf'. Jim Trevor may have done his best, but he was at the same time defying the Old Wolf to do his worst, and in the end the Old Wolf has to admit defeat: Jim is taken on as another pilot's cub – that is literally the word used – he is accepted as a 'prentice pilot. Doubts about morals increase if we consider the remaining stories in *Land And Sea Tales*.

'An English School' is interesting today chiefly as a scrap of autobiography and as the seed-bed of *Stalky & Co.*: written in 1893 it contains unimproved versions of tales that were to figure largely in the book. One interesting difference is that Beresford (not yet McTurk) seems to have been the leader, rather than Stalky, in some of the boys' illicit enterprises. And what enterprises they were! B-P, remembering his own schooldays, may have smiled at them indulgently, but illicit smoking – insolence to schoolmasters – pouring melted bacon fat over smaller boys' heads – selling your wardrobe, pawning your watch – writing low satirical comments on schoolfellows in the school magazine – stealing apples and pheasants' eggs and geese from neighbouring estates, at the risk of gunfire from gamekeepers – fighting duels with saloon-pistols in the sand-dunes: was this really the sort of thing that the Scouts wanted to encourage? True, Kipling insisted that the spirit of the school was good, and led to devoted service in India and elsewhere; but young minds might well mistake the message.

Even if the Chief Scout discounted all this because Kipling was sound on amateur acting (good) and cadet corps (bad), what about the tale simply entitled 'Stalky'? It has since come to figure in *The Complete Stalky & Co.* and it is hard to see why Kipling excluded it from the original volume, unless it was that 'In Ambush', that tale which is all sunshine, summer breezes and flowering gorse, made an exceptionally fine opener. 'Stalky' is all chill rain, but serves very well in *Land And Sea Tales*. But even Kipling seems to have had doubts:

A certain amount of it, I am sorry to say, is founded on fact, though that is no recommendation; and the only moral that

I can see in it is, that when for any reason you happen to get
into a tight place, you have a better chance of coming out of
it comfortably if you keep your head than if you get excited
and don't stop to think. (p. 129.)

A familiar Kipling moral. But the story, concerning cattle-lifting
and set-tos with farmers and, worst of all, the tormenting of poor
animals with a pea-shooter, all without a shred of punishment or
repentance, positively seems to encourage the precise sort of
behaviour which all scoutmasters with camps to run must absol-
utely deplore.

But then *Stalky & Co.* is essentially a subversive book and
this escape from its pages could hardly be different. What,
however, are we to make of the last remaining story in *Land
And Sea Tales*, the only prose work expressly composed for it,
and the only one concerned with the Boy Scouts themselves?
Kipling can offer no excuse here. He is recalling no boyhood
pranks of his own; he is a venerated, respectable author of the
utmost dignity. Yet he is still Beetle at heart, and when chal-
lenged by the sight of anything so virtuous as the Boy Scout
movement must be as disrespectful as ever.

I really cannot overstate the pleasure I derive from 'His Gift'.
Careful reading shows it to be an intelligent and sensitive tribute
to the possibilities of Scouting; but its humour derives from the
unspoken knowledge shared between author and reader that
in life Scouting often does not realise its potential: it can be
conventional, boring and third-rate. The manner in which fat,
lazy, clumsy and unintelligent William Glasse Sawyer turns the
tables on his world – on his persecutor, the Prawn, on his Scout
Troop, and even on his uncle, who is probably the source of
half his unhappiness – must give joy to every unregenerate heart
(the regenerate never get much out of Kipling). The means by
which William achieves his revenge is also delightful, not least
because of the delicate humour, the flickering rhetoric, with
which Kipling makes his points:

'Yes, a good cook,' Mr Marsh went on reminiscently, 'even
on Board of Trade allowance, 'as brought many a ship to
port that 'ud otherwise 'ave mutinied on the 'igh seas.' ...
He filled an ancient pipe with eloquent tobacco, and while

William scoured the pan, he held forth on the art and science and mystery of cooking as inspiredly as Mr. Jorrocks, Master of Foxhounds, had lectured upon the Chase. The burden of his song was Power – power which, striking directly at the stomach of man, makes the rudest polite, not to say syco-phantic, towards a good cook, whether at sea, in camp, in the face of war, or (here he embellished his text with personal experiences) the crowded competitive cities where a good meal was as rare, he declared, as silk pyjamas in a pigsty. 'An' mark you,' he concluded, 'three times a day the 'aughtiest and most overbearin' of 'em all 'ave to come crawling to you for a round belly-full. Put *that* in your pipe and smoke it out, young Sherlock!'

He unloosed his sacrificial apron and rolled away.

The Boy Scout is used to strangers who give him good advice on the smallest provocation; but strangers who fill you up with bacon and eggs and ginger-beer are few.[1]

On first reading, 'His Gift' seems entirely subversive, an effect largely wrought by its likeness to a Stalky story, particularly to 'In Ambush': the scene where William lies hidden in the fern and eavesdrops on Mr Marsh's encounter with The Prawn recalls both Stalky & Co's lair in the furze and the immortal scene in which Colonel Dabney berates Foxy, King and Prout while the boys lie hidden in the cottage close at hand. But closer examination reveals important differences. William's Scout-master, for instance, plays a small, essential, purely beneficial part in the tale: he sees what is happening to William, and by inviting Mr Marsh to re-visit the camp-fire makes sure that the process of salvation is completed. Nor is William an outlaw, like Stalky, Beetle and McTurk: by the end of his story he is the most respected member of his troop, thanks to his gift for cooking. Nor does Kipling for a moment suggest that dis-covering his vocation is going to turn William into a soldier of the Queen. His sole concern is to show how, through Scouting and a little good luck, a Mug, an unprofitable person, a Mark A Ass, can be turned into a happy, useful citizen – just as Baden-Powell proclaimed. In short, the whole story is an embodiment

[1] *Land And Sea Tales*, pp. 92–3.

of the attitudes urged by *Scouting For Boys* (which does not neglect cooking). It is one more testimony of Kipling's astonishing gift for entering and re-creating a world of which he had little first-hand knowledge. In this case he may have got his second-hand knowledge from the Scout he encountered at the Posse of Welcome. It would have been like him to turn the boy inside out.

'His Gift', then, if it subverts anything, subverts the military approach to Scouting we find in most of the other tales. Kipling cannot have cared. The story breathes good humour, and is happily rounded off by a parody of Chaucer, the 'Prologue To The Master-Cook's Tale' which follows 'His Gift'. As a prologue, it would have come better before the story, rather than after it; but so placed it would have diminished the reader's pleasant surprise when he begins to learn what William's gift is. Taken together, verses and tale are well up to the standard of anything in *Debits And Credits*, on which Kipling was working at the same time; and in view of the theme, and the allusions to Mrs Glasse and Mr Jorrocks, they would have appeared very suitably in that volume, and have been better known if they had. But they were dedicated to the Scouts and Guides, and *Land And Sea Tales* was their proper home.

B-P's acknowledgment of this splendid gift, if one was written, does not appear to survive; but we can infer that it was warm from the next Scout rally involving Kipling. In the following year, 1924, in connection with the Imperial Exhibition at Wembley, a great Imperial Boy Scout Jamboree was held. Once more Kipling's influence was much in evidence: 630 Scouts from Sussex enacted what they called 'Puck's Pageant of the march of time through Sussex', which included the singing of many of Kipling's songs (presumably from *Puck Of Pook's Hill* and *Rewards And Fairies*) 'set to music for this occasion only by permission of the author'.[1] And here was a chance to make good the blunder of 1922. Wednesday, 6 August, was to be Wolf Cub Day, and be presided over by the Duke of York. With him in his box on that occasion were Mr and Mrs Rudyard Kipling (he again in top hat) who now at last were able to savour in full splendour B-P's adaptation of the *Jungle Books*, for beneath

[1] *The Scouter*, August 1924, p. 286.

them 6,100 Cubs performed the jungle dances and scenes from Mowgli's story. There is nothing on the point in the official records, but it would have been a strange sort of Cubs' Day if a Howl had not been howled, and a member of the Kipling Society, who was then a child living near Wembley, remembers being told that there was indeed a Howl. So no doubt Kipling came away satisfied.

That seems to have been the end of his direct involvement with the movement. His Commissionership seems to have been purely honorary: there is no record of his attending any meetings of the Scout Council, and he was ageing fast. But he was not forgotten. B-P in 1932 sent him a French rendering of the Jungle story passages of the *Wolf Cubs Handbook*; and when the news of his death came wrote a glowing tribute which appeared in *The Scouter* of March 1936. It accurately expresses B-P's feelings about Kipling and, perhaps, some of the limits of his perceptions:

> Through the death of Rudyard Kipling the Empire has lost a great upholder, and our Movement has lost a true and valued friend. From its earliest days Scouting was heartily encouraged by him ... he had practically been a lifelong friend to me, and I shall sorely miss his cheery, clever and helpful personality.
>
> But the memory of him will live, not only as one of the greatest of our modern authors, but also as a whole-hearted patriot who saw the value of an united Empire as a force for the peace and prosperity of our race.
>
> May his example be an inspiration to others, and may he rest in peace.

In the same issue of *The Scouter* there appeared an article setting out the details of a new jungle dance, 'Dance of the Death of Shere Khan'. Somebody's soul, undoubtedly, still went marching on.

INDEX